Mapping Our Nation

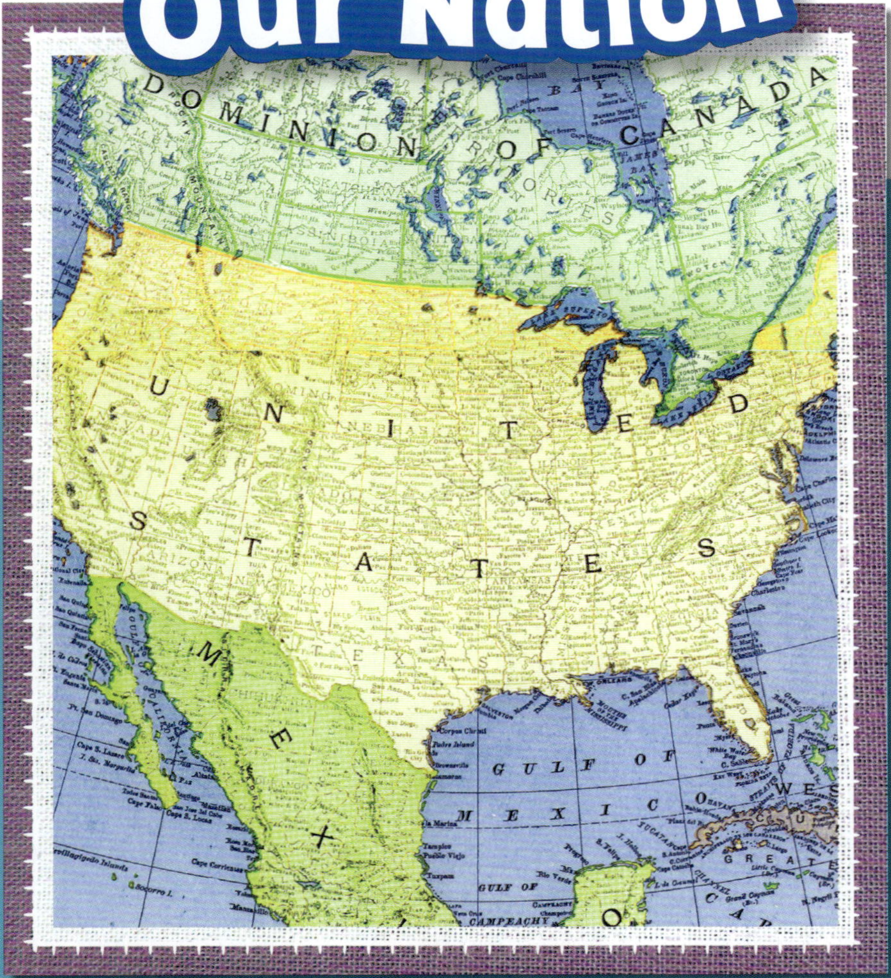

Sandy Phan

Consultants

Shelley Scudder
Gifted Education Teacher
Broward County Schools

Caryn Williams, M.S.Ed.
Madison County Schools
Huntsville, AL

Publishing Credits

Conni Medina, M.A.Ed., *Managing Editor*
Lee Aucoin, *Creative Director*
Torrey Maloof, *Editor*
Marissa Rodriguez, *Designer*
Stephanie Reid, *Photo Editor*
Rachelle Cracchiolo, M.S.Ed., *Publisher*

Image Credits: pp. 25, 28, 29(top) Alamy; p. 29(bottom) Blake S.; p. 26–27 Digital Wisdom; pp. 10–11, 14–15, 18(top), 21, 24, 26(left) iStockphoto; p. 8 Map Store; p. 6–7 Mapping Specialists; pp. 12, 14, 16, 18(bottom), 22(top) Stephanie Reid; All other images Shutterstock.

Teacher Created Materials
5301 Oceanus Drive
Huntington Beach, CA 92649-1030
http://www.tcmpub.com

ISBN 978-1-4333-6999-5

Printed by: 590835
Printed in: China

Table of Contents

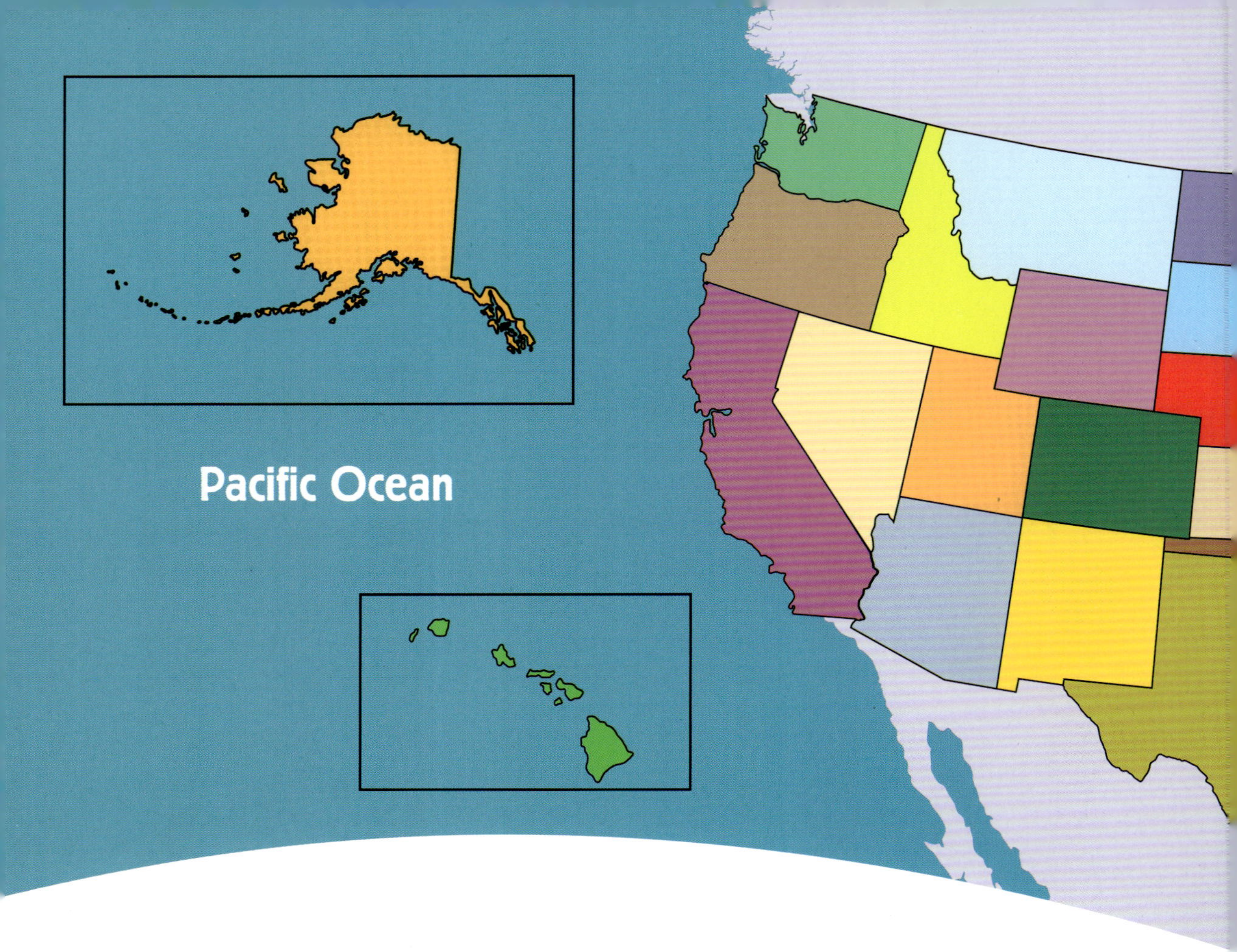

Using Maps

The United States is huge! It stretches from the Pacific Ocean to the Atlantic Ocean. It is made up of 50 states. Some of the states are larger than whole countries!

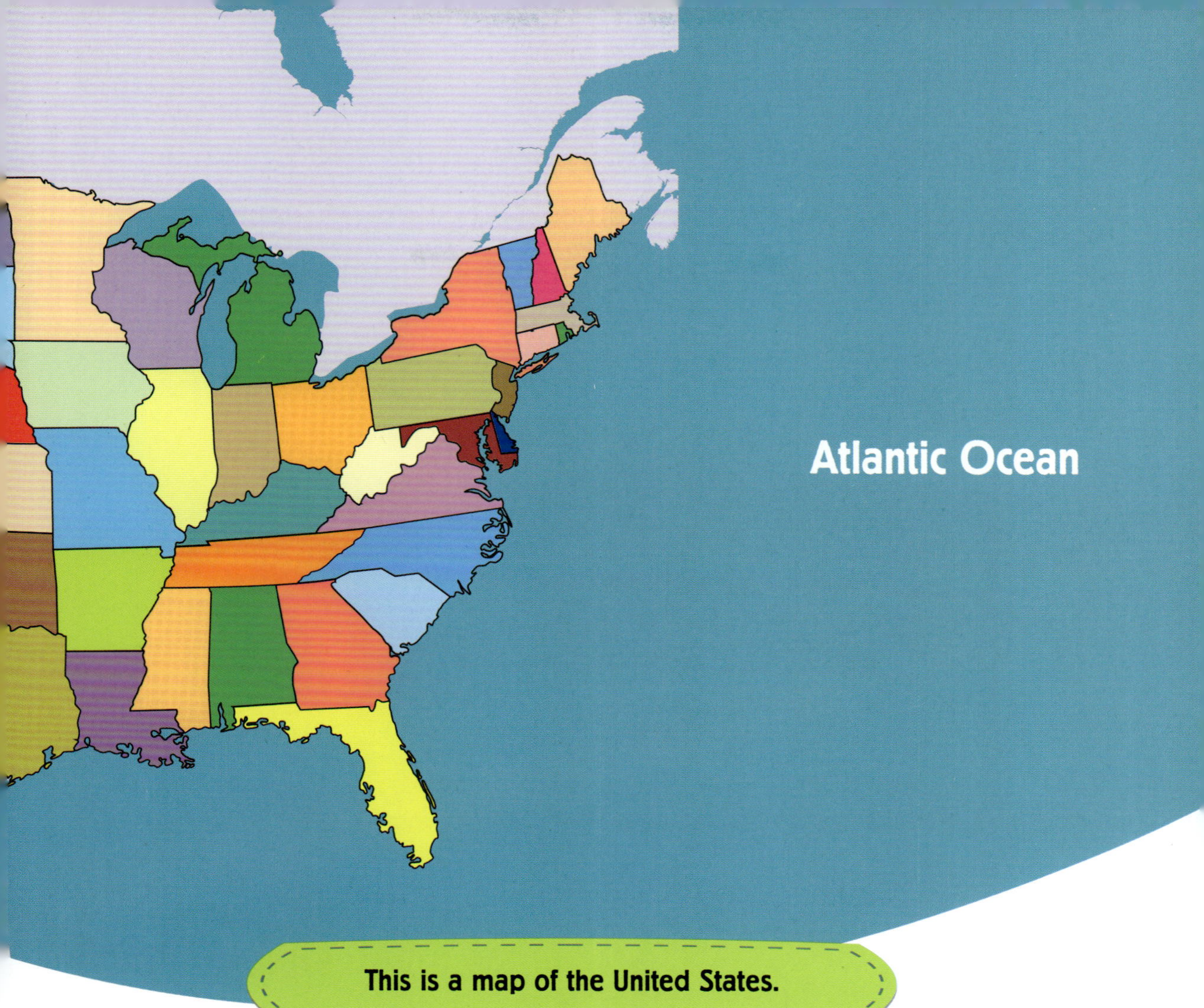

This is a map of the United States.

We can use maps to learn about our nation. Maps help us see the shape of the land. Maps also show us important places. Let's explore our nation!

There are tools to help us read maps. The legend, or key, explains the symbols, lines, and colors on a map. A compass rose shows the four directions: north, south, east, and west.

This is a legend, or key.

This is a compass rose.

This is a scale.

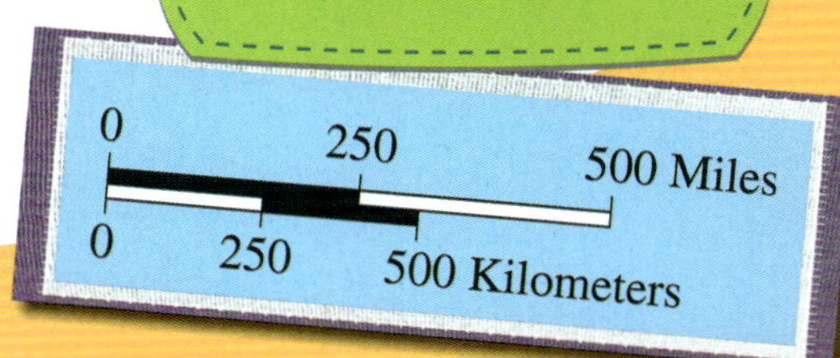

Another tool is the scale. It helps us measure distances on a map. If you know how to use these tools, you can read any map!

This map shows our nation's rivers and mountains.

Types of Maps

There are many types of maps. **Physical maps** show water such as rivers and lakes. They also show **landforms**. These are natural features on Earth's surface. Mountains, deserts, and plains are landforms.

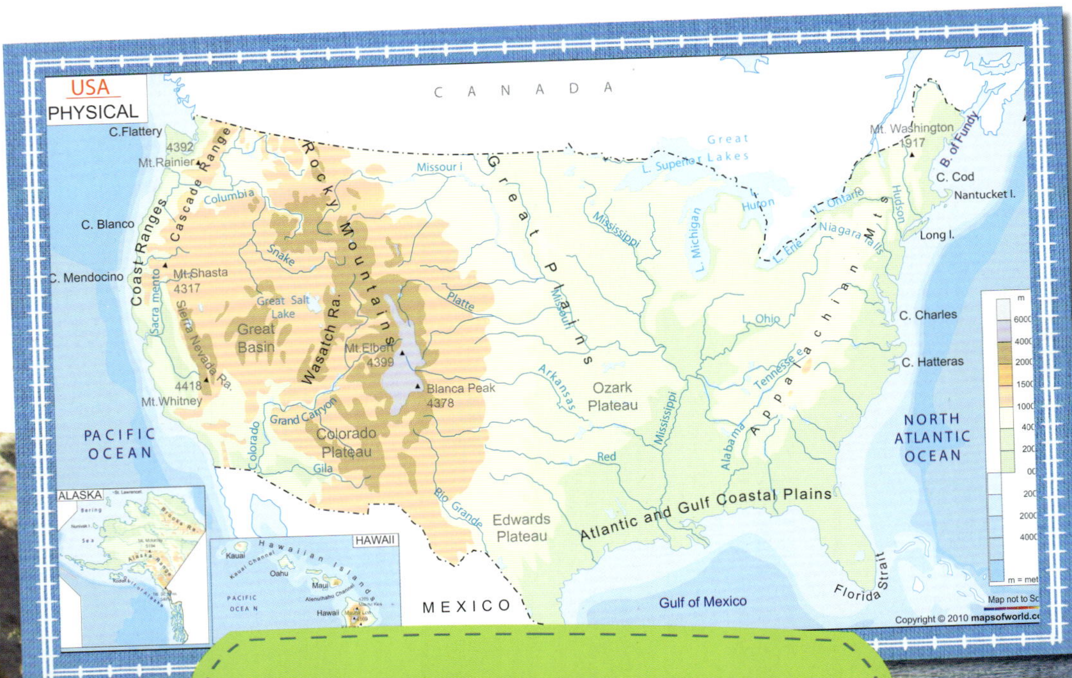

This is a physical map of the United States.

Elevation (el-uh-VEY-shuhn) is the height of a place. A mountain has a higher elevation than a desert. Some physical maps show elevation.

Longest River

The Missouri (mi-ZOOR-ee) River is the longest river in the United States. It is 2,540 miles long. It starts in Montana. It ends in Missouri. There, it joins the Mississippi River.

This is the Missouri River.

Another type of map is a **political map**. A political map shows the borders between places. It shows how people have split up the land.

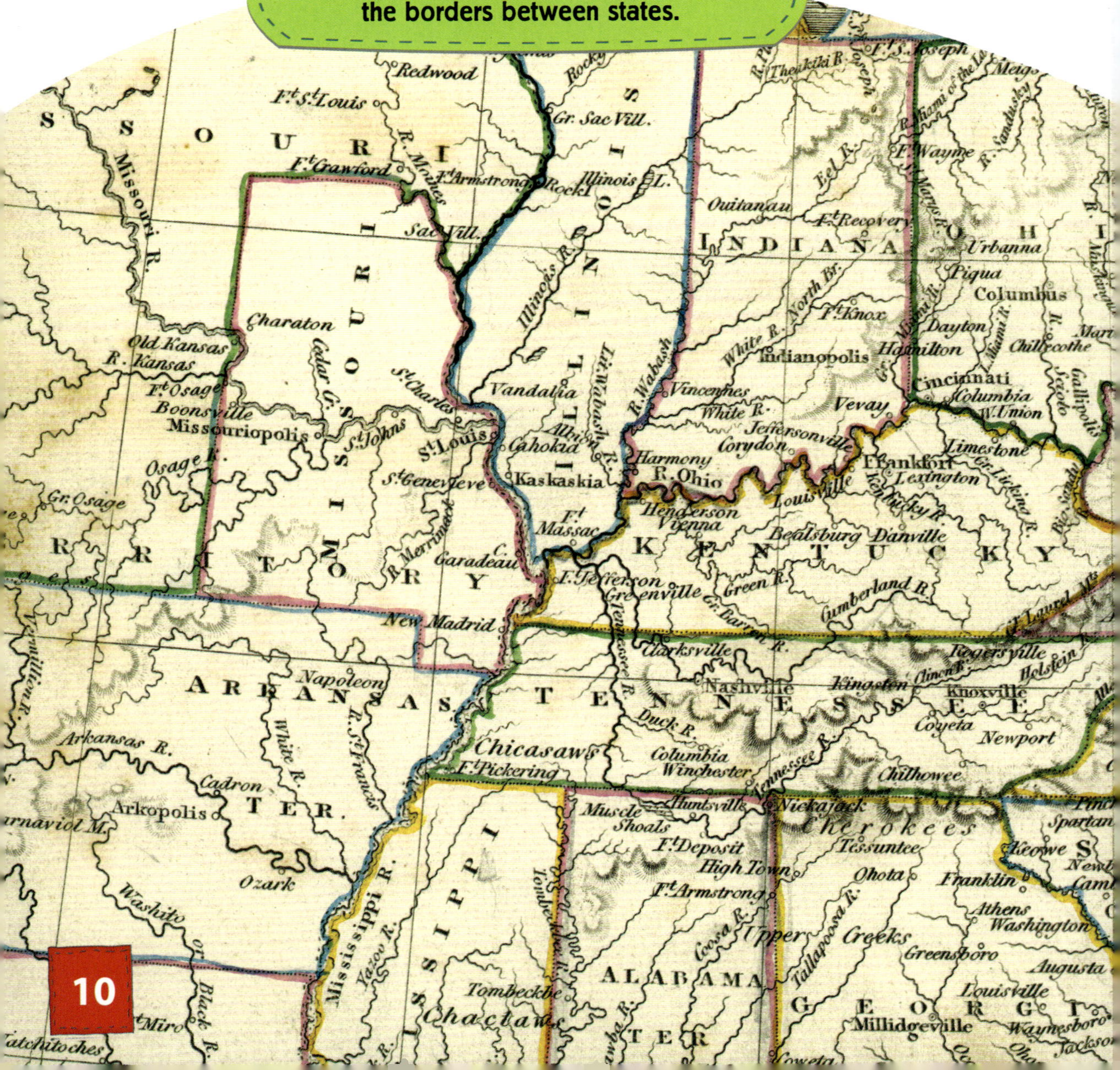

Colors on this old map show the borders between states.

A political map of the United States shows the 50 states. Sometimes, it shows their capitals, too. Each state is like a puzzle piece. These pieces form a picture of our nation.

Capital Cities

Each state has a capital city. This city is where the government (GUHV-ern-muhnt) has its main offices. Do you know your state's capital city?

This is a political map of the United States.

A **thematic map** shows how people or things are spread out over a place. It may show the number of people who live in an area.

A thematic map may also show the food that is grown in that area. It may show the roads on which people travel, too.

This thematic map shows major roads in the United States.

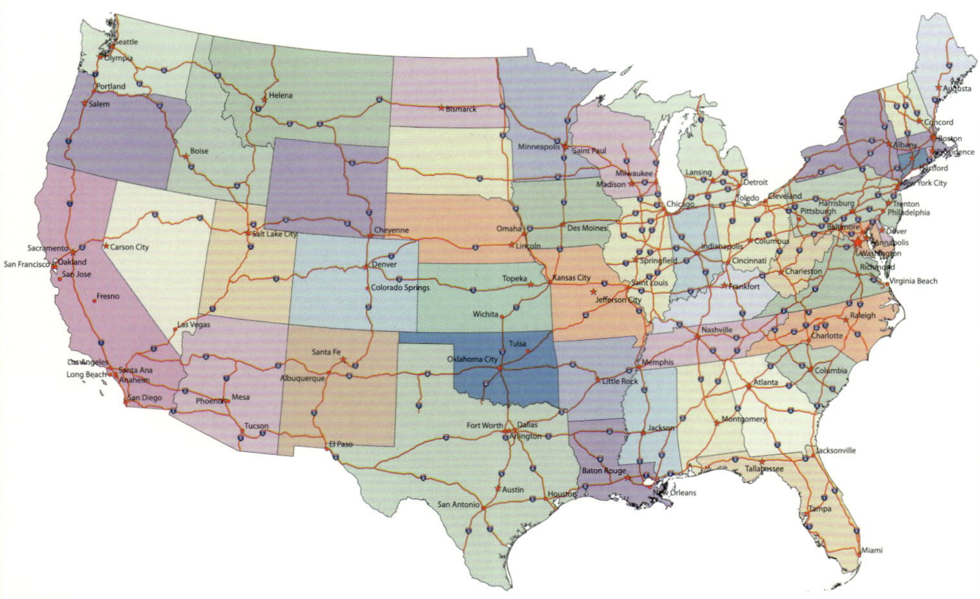

Regions

A **region** is an area of land. It has its own features. These features set it apart from other areas around it.

These are the four regions of the United States.

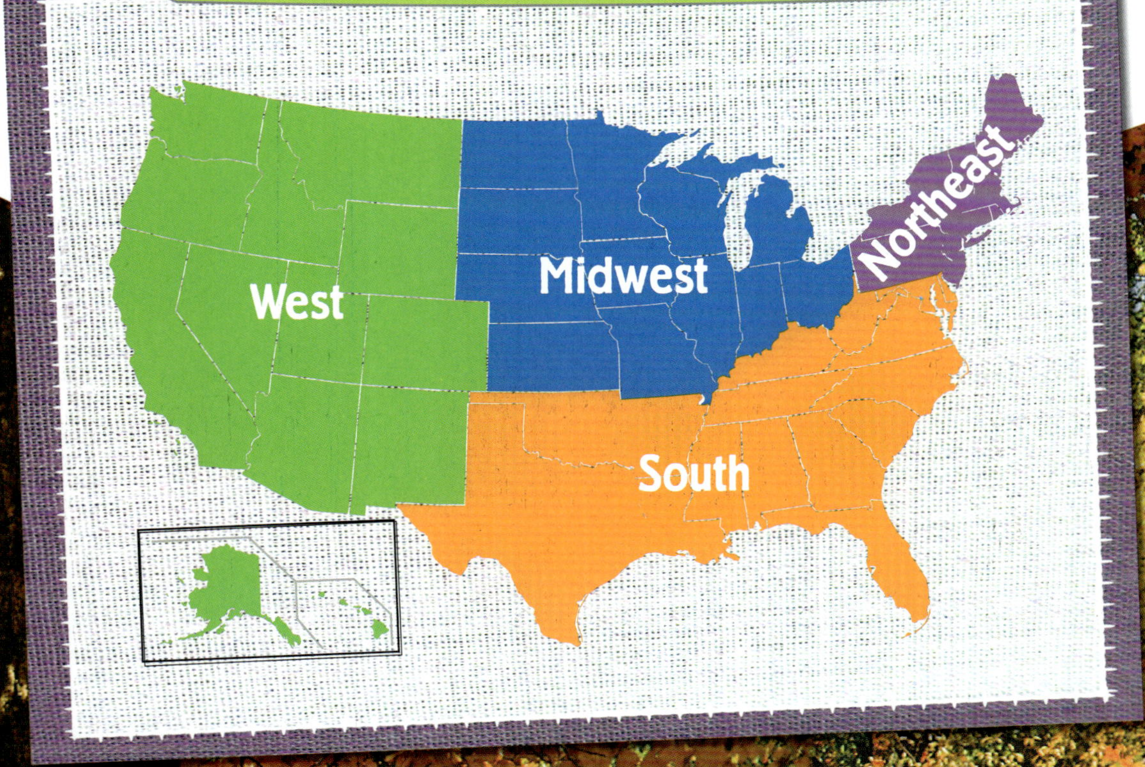

A region may have a certain **climate**, or weather pattern. Or, maybe a special type of animal lives there. Each region has its own unique traits.

This is the Northeast region.

Four Regions

The United States can be split many different ways. One way is to split it into four regions. These four regions are the Northeast, the South, the Midwest, and the West. In which region do you live?

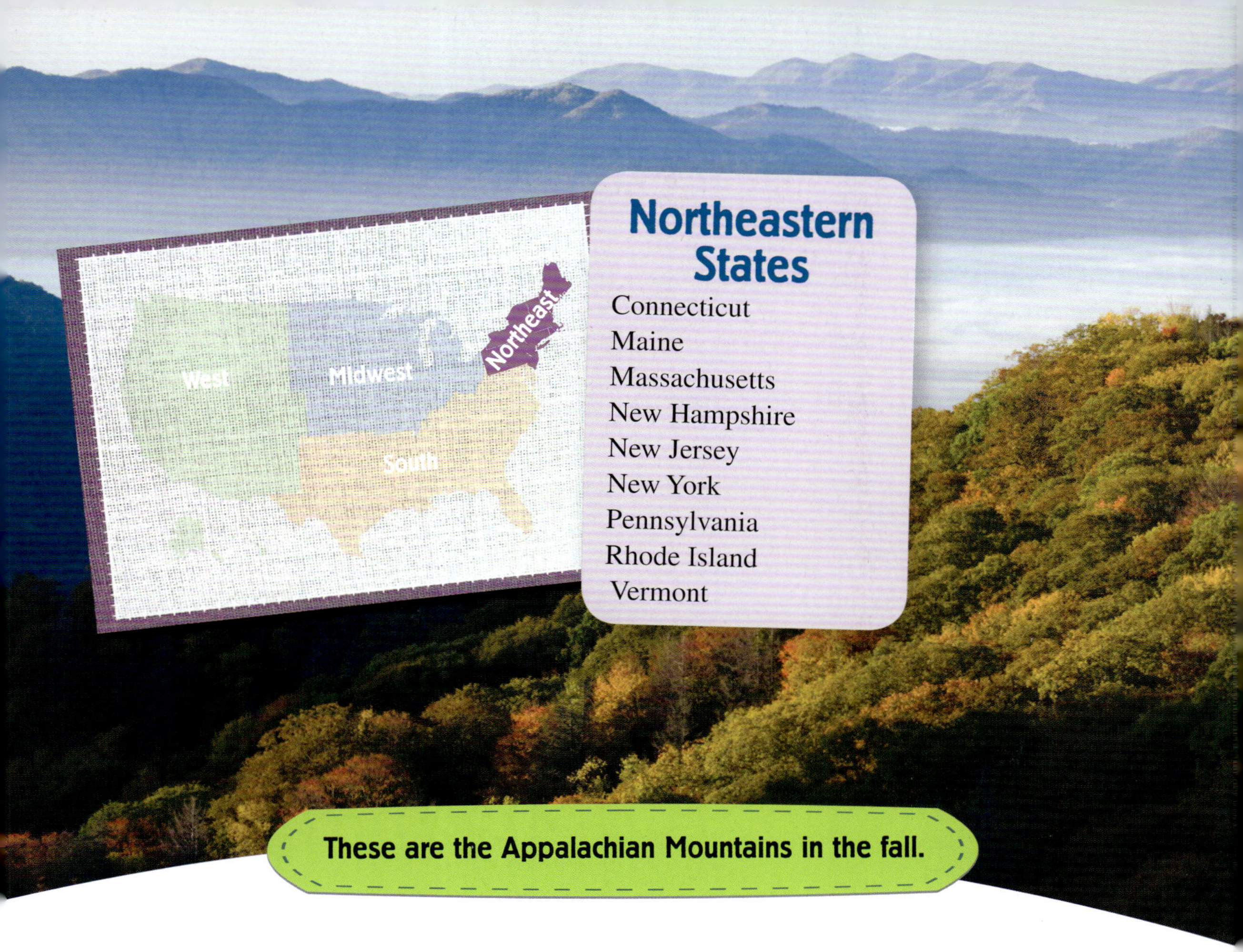

Northeastern States

Connecticut
Maine
Massachusetts
New Hampshire
New Jersey
New York
Pennsylvania
Rhode Island
Vermont

These are the Appalachian Mountains in the fall.

The Northeast

There are nine states in the Northeast region. It has cold, snowy winters. It has hot summers. The leaves turn beautiful colors in the fall. And the spring brings rain showers.

Big City!

The largest city in the United States is located in the Northeast region. It is New York City!

New York City

The Northeast region is also known for its Appalachian (ap-uh-LEY-chuhn) Mountains. These are some of the oldest mountains on Earth.

The South

There are 16 states in the South. Most of the states in this region have warm climates. Some areas are always covered in water. These areas are called *swamps*. Many swamps have alligators!

Do you see the alligator in the swamp?

Southern States

Alabama
Arkansas
Delaware
Florida
Georgia
Kentucky
Louisiana
Maryland
Mississippi
North Carolina
Oklahoma
South Carolina
Tennessee
Texas
Virginia
West Virginia

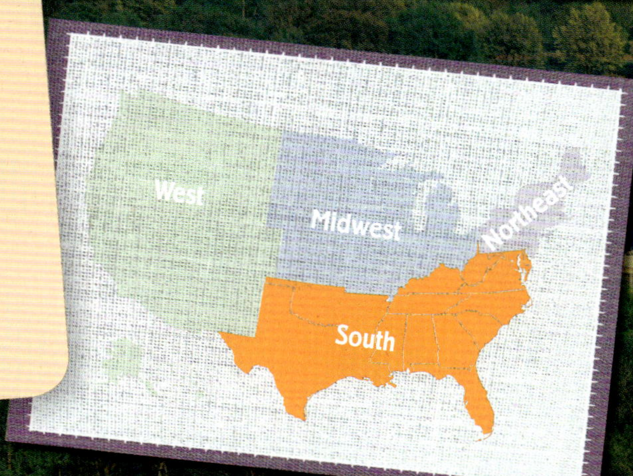

There are large rivers in this region that help farmers grow crops. Cotton, rice, and citrus fruits all grow well in the South.

Our Nation's Capital

Did you know that our nation's capital is in the South? Washington, DC, is located on the Potomac (puh-TOH-muhk) River by Maryland and Virginia.

Washington, DC

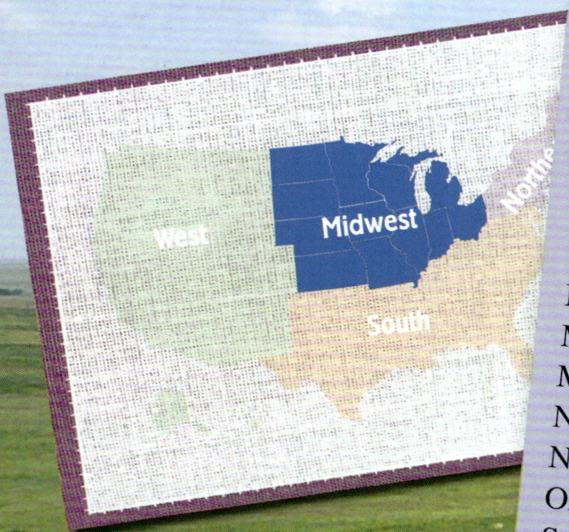

Midwestern States

Illinois
Indiana
Iowa
Kansas
Michigan
Minnesota
Missouri
Nebraska
North Dakota
Ohio
South Dakota
Wisconsin

Out on the Farm

The Midwest has many farms. These farms mainly grow crops such as wheat, oats, and corn.

These are the Great Plains.

The Midwest

There are 12 states in the Midwest region. The climate is mostly dry. The Great Plains are in this region. This is a large, flat area of land. It is covered in grasses.

This map shows the Great Lakes.

The Great Lakes are also in this region. These freshwater lakes take up over 94,000 square miles! Many fish such as salmon and trout live in the lakes.

The West

A large area of land makes up the West. There are 13 states in this region. Their climates vary. Oregon is rainy and foggy. Colorado can be very cold. And Arizona can get very hot.

Western States

Alaska
Arizona
California
Colorado
Hawaii
Idaho
Montana
Nevada
New Mexico
Oregon
Utah
Washington
Wyoming

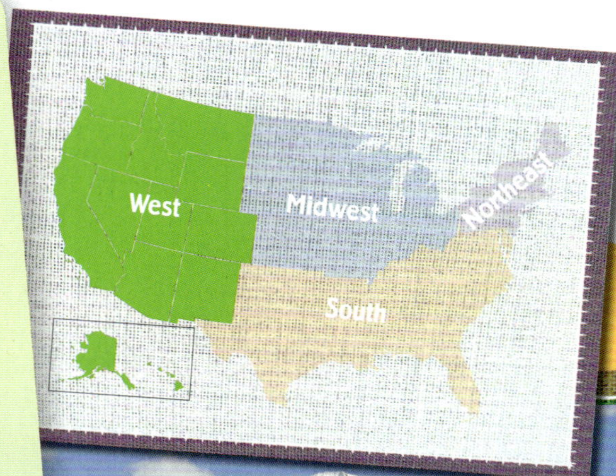

This is a glacier in Alaska.

There are deserts and beaches in the West. There are also mountains. There are **glaciers** (GLEY-sherz) in Alaska. And Hawaii (huh-WAHY-ee) has volcanoes!

Grand Canyon

Long ago, the Colorado River cut through an area of Arizona to create a deep valley. Today, this valley is called the Grand Canyon. It is over 270 miles long!

This is the Grand Canyon.

Modern Maps

A book of maps is called an **atlas**. An atlas can help you learn more about an area. It has facts and pictures about different places.

This is an atlas from 1879.

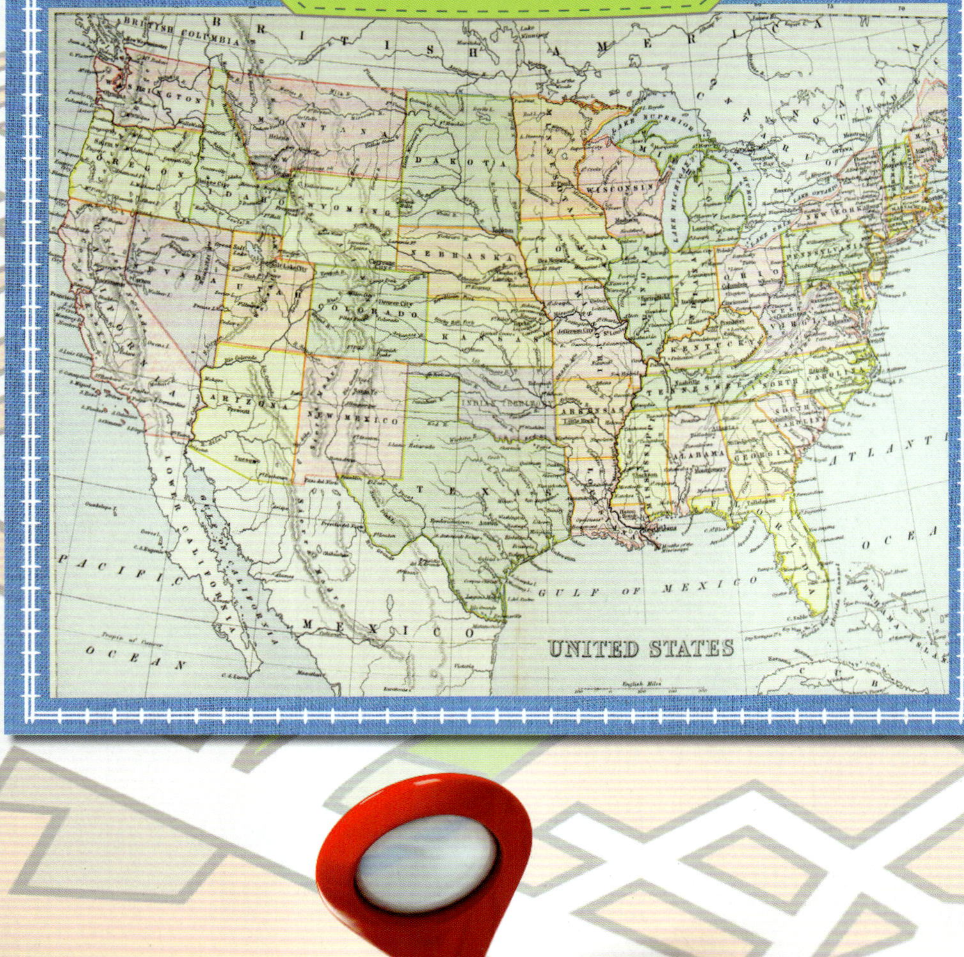

Today, we can look at maps on computers. Some of these maps are **interactive**. This means that you can click on the maps to learn more about places in our nation.

Images from Space

Google Earth is a 3-D interactive map of our planet. The map is made from pictures taken by machines (muh-SHEENZ) in space called *satellites*. Google Earth has pictures, videos, and other great tools to help you learn.

This woman is using Google Earth on a tablet.

One Nation

Maps of the United States are important. Maps show the landforms on which we live. They show the rivers and lakes that help us grow food. They show the roads on which we travel.

Kilauea Volcano, Hawaii

Rocky Mountains, Colorado

Maps show us how and why each region is different. But they also show us how these regions are all part of one nation.

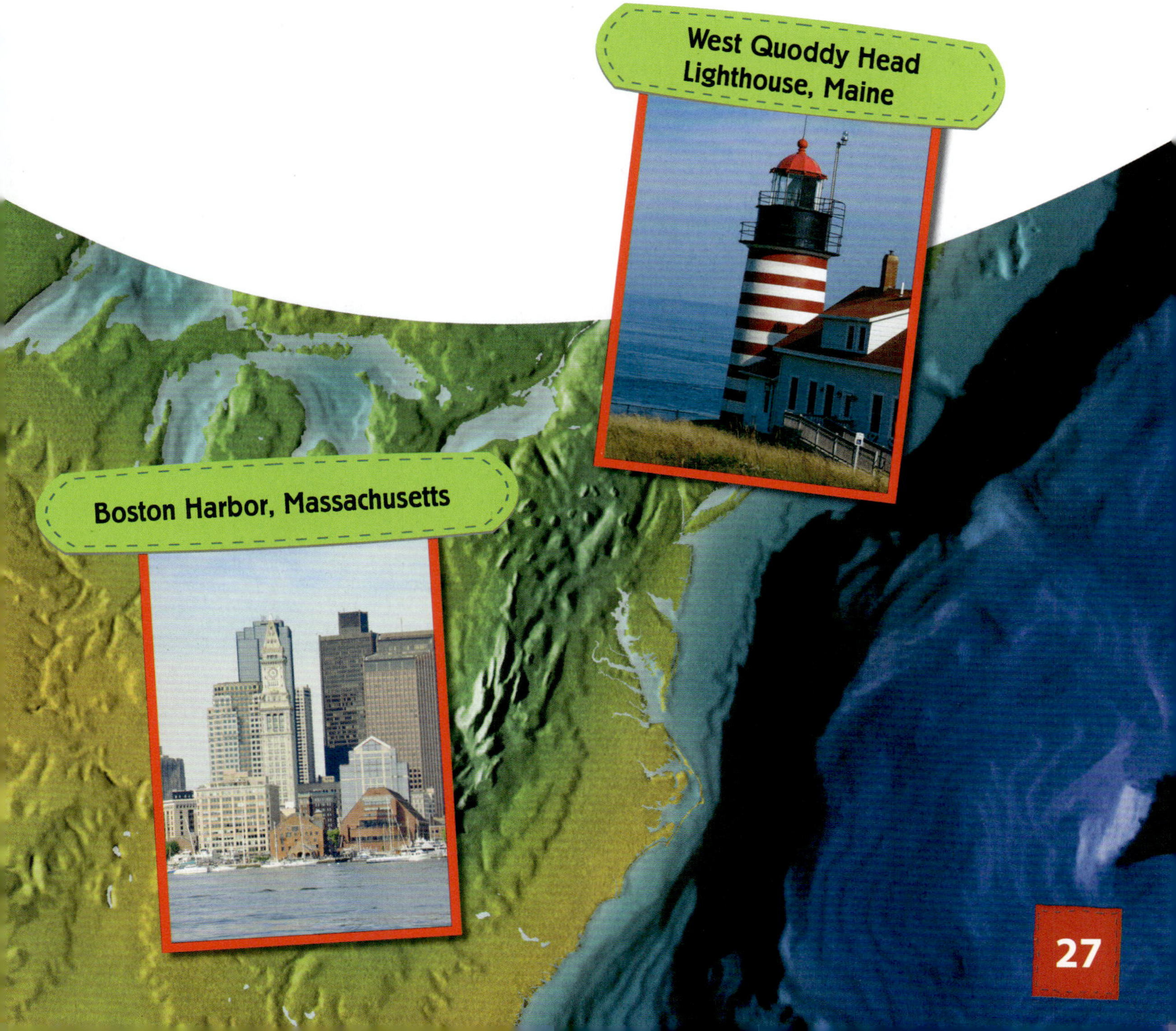

Make It!

You can make maps, too. Make a map of the United States. It can be any kind of map. It may show where sports teams play or where your family members live. Share your map with your friends.

This boy is making a map that shows all the places his family members live.

This girl is making a map that shows the states she has visited.

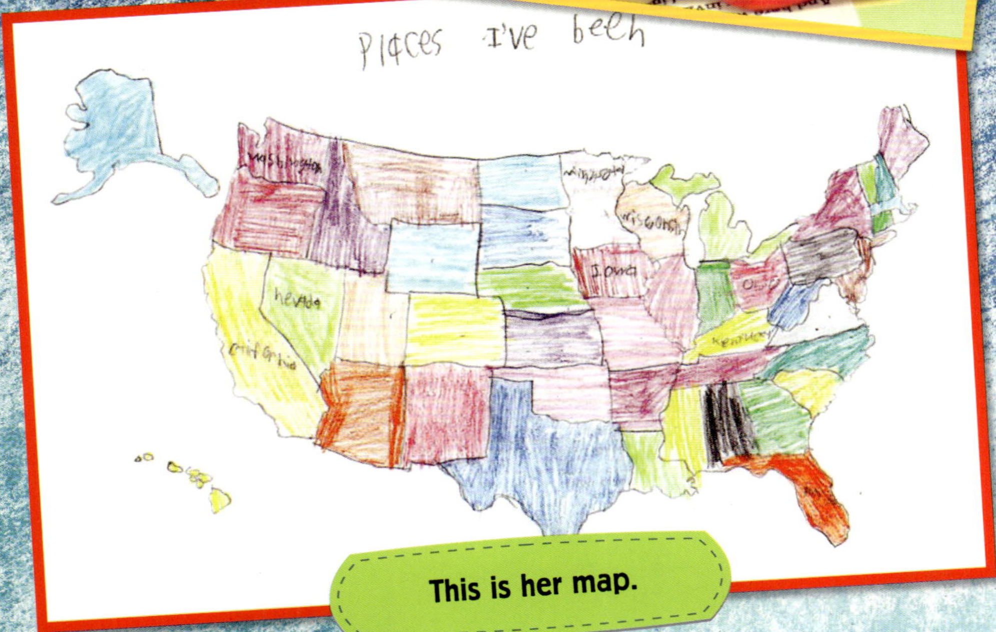

This is her map.

Glossary

atlas—a book of maps

climate—weather patterns in a certain region

elevation—the height of a place

glaciers—very large pieces of ice that move slowly over a wide area of land

interactive—made to respond to the actions of a person

landforms—natural land features on Earth's surface, such as mountains or plains

physical maps—maps that show a place's land and water

political map—a map that shows how people have split up the land

region—a part of an area that is different from other parts in some way

thematic map—a map that shows a certain subject or theme of one area

Index

Your Turn!

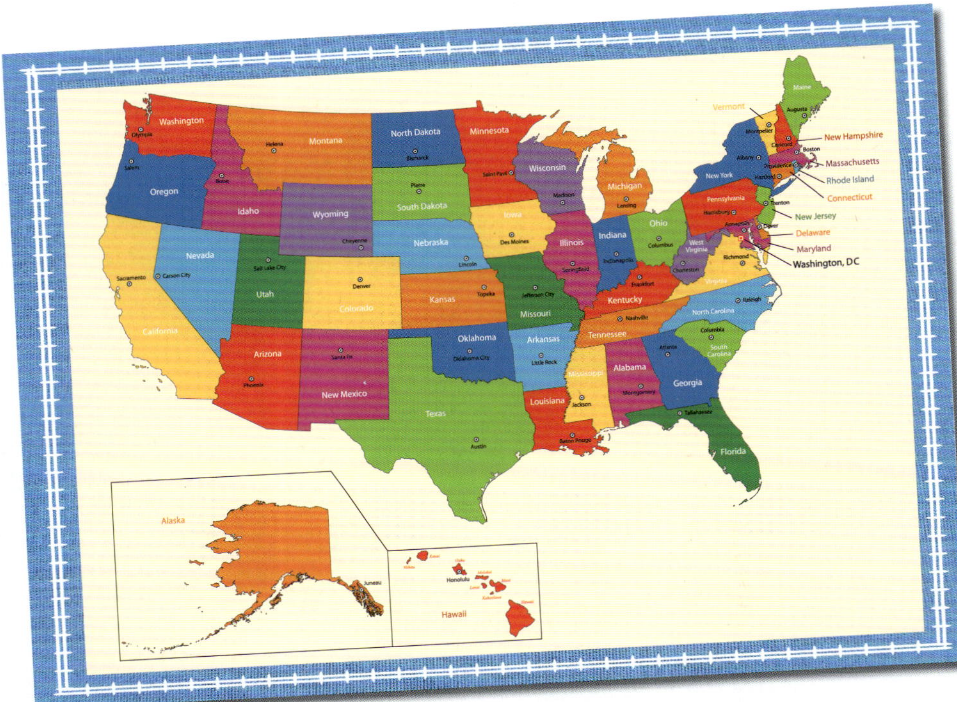

You Are Here

This is a political map of the United States. It shows all 50 states and their capitals. In which state do you live? In which region is it? List two features of that region.